Animals

Horses

by Nick Rebman

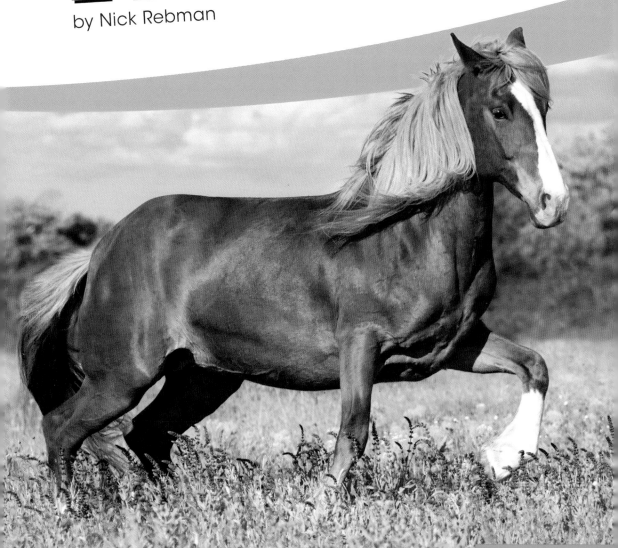

FOCUS READERS

www.focusreaders.com

Focus Readers is distributed by North Star Editions:
sales@northstareditions.com | 888-417-0195

Produced for Focus Readers by Red Line Editorial.

Photographs ©: Callipso/Shutterstock Images, cover, 1; Eduard Kyslynskyy/Shutterstock Images, 4; mariait/Shutterstock Images, 7, 9, 16 (top right); Emir Memedovski/iStockphoto, 11; Edoma/Shutterstock Images, 13, 16 (bottom left); Nicole Ciscato/Shutterstock Images, 15; MaxyM/Shutterstock Images, 16 (top left); Mikhail Pogosov/Shutterstock Images, 16 (bottom right)

ISBN
978-1-63517-850-0 (hardcover)
978-1-63517-951-4 (paperback)
978-1-64185-154-1 (ebook pdf)
978-1-64185-053-7 (hosted ebook)

Library of Congress Control Number: 2018931099

Printed in the United States of America
Mankato, MN
May, 2018

About the Author

Nick Rebman enjoys reading, drawing, and traveling to places where he doesn't speak the language. He lives in Minnesota.

Table of Contents

Horses

Horses can be

many colors.

Some are white.

Some are brown.

Some are black.

A horse has four legs.

A horse has a **tail**.

A horse has a **mane**.

A mane is hair on the head
and neck.

mane

leg

tail

Behavior

Horses live in groups.

Horses can run fast.

Horses can run far.

Many horses live on **farms**.

People take care of them.

Food

Horses eat **hay**.

Hay is dry grass.

Horses also need lots
of water.

Horses are strong.

They can live for 30 years.

Glossary

farms

mane

hay

tail

Index